Maureen Attwooll (née Boddy) lives in Weymouth and is the co-author of several books on the town's history, including *Weymouth, An Illustrated History* (1983), *Seaside Weymouth* (1989), and *Weymouth and Portland at War* (1993). She has also been researching Dorset's shipwrecks for a number of years and she compiled and published one of the first definitive lists of Dorset wrecks. Her illustrated talks on the subject are well-known.

Following page
The *Avalanche* and *Forest* disaster, 1877: the lines that follow are from a contemporary poem describing Portland fishermen bringing the survivors ashore.

The Chesil beachmen saw
The storm tossed boat draw near
They knew that boat once in the break
Each man would need a bier.
Swiftly a lerret's launched
Manned by a gallant seven
Brave Shaddock means the men to save
Or go himself to Heaven.
Too great the task for one
He hails their friends on shore
Another lerret's quickly launched
Manned by seven brave men more.
And soon the shipwrecked crew
Are safe upon the beach
God grant those gallant Chesil men
May always be in reach.

DISCOVER DORSET

SHIPWRECKS

MAUREEN ATTWOOLL

THE DOVECOTE PRESS

Portland's Newfoundland 'Sea Dogs' or 'Rescue Dogs'
were fearless in rough seas. As well as saving lives, they
were trained to retrieve small barrels of contraband spirits
hidden offshore by local smugglers. The breed has been
extinct on the Island since the last century.

First published in 1998 by The Dovecote Press Ltd
Stanbridge, Wimborne, Dorset BH21 4JD

ISBN 1 874336 59 8

Series designed by Humphrey Stone

Typeset in Sabon by The Typesetting Bureau
Wimborne, Dorset
Printed and bound by Baskerville Press, Salisbury, Wiltshire

A CIP catalogue record for this book is available
from the British Library

1 3 5 7 9 8 6 4 2

CONTENTS

SHIP ASHORE

Thousands of ships and lives have been lost in the English Channel since man first sailed this dangerous and busy seaway. Vessels of every description have foundered on the rocks, ledges, beaches and bays which lie between Poole Harbour and Lyme Regis – victims to storm, fog, fire, human error and war. At best, if a stranded vessel can be refloated, the result is a delayed voyage. At worst, a ship, its crew, passengers and cargo are lost. There is nothing remotely romantic about a shipwreck, yet crowds of sightseers turn out to view a vessel in distress, and divers find fascination in searching out and exploring wrecks which have gone down offshore.

Our ancestors showed a keen interest in shipwrecks along the Dorset coast. Passive onlookers they were not. Ships cast ashore and split open by wave and storm spewed out their cargoes for all to see and the locals soon arrived in force to plunder and to steal. A really good wreck might yield up gold, silver and other valuables, but even in a more modest cargo there was always something worth taking. Wood, ropes, household goods, fruit and wine were useful supplements to the meagre incomes of the labouring poor. And it was not only the poor who gathered on the beaches – practically everyone in the neighbourhood was involved in this profitable, if illegal, 'industry' and stolen goods were spirited away up country through a

Top left A modern tragedy: the loss of the ketch *Reliance* at Cave Hole, Portland, in 1949. Her crew of two had been hoping to make a fresh start abroad on a 'paradise isle' but had been troubled by heavy weather since the start of the voyage from Fleetwood. Frank Davison died when the vessel foundered at Portland. His wife Ann survived and of her ordeal she said: 'I did not look back at the sea. I knew I had beaten the sea for myself, but only for myself. Everything else the sea won from me.'

Left Providing almost a classic shipwreck picture, the rice-laden barquentine *Ehen* stranded in cottonwool fog at Mutton Cove, Portland on 21st April, 1890. All on board were saved, but the vessel became a total loss.

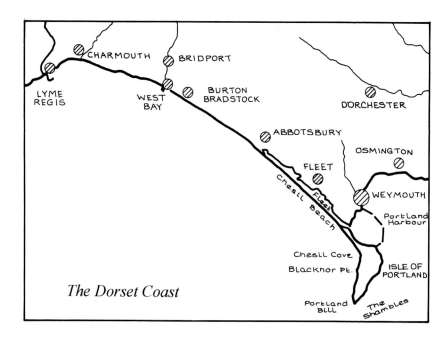

The Dorset Coast

network of contacts in the inland villages and towns to be sold later when the hue and cry died down.

Rights of Wreck were anciently claimed by the Crown, although it was not uncommon for them to be granted to a Lord of the Manor, church or monastery in lieu of payment for some service to the crown. Local people, with their long history of evading the laws regarding piracy and smuggling, simply helped themselves to the contents of shipwrecked vessels and hoped to avoid being found out. Law enforcement at the scene of a wreck was an almost impossible task for a handful of revenue officers and constables.

What exactly constituted a 'Wreck' was another legal nicety which was conveniently overlooked. A thirteenth century statute decreed 'that where a Man, a Dog or a Cat escape quick out of the Ship, that such Ship nor Barge, nor any Thing within them, shall be adjudged Wreck'. If there were any survivors as described, the ship and cargo still rightfully belonged to the original owners who were entitled to lay claim to their goods 'within a Year and a Day'. This law offered little comfort to a cold, exhausted crew huddled on shore, whose

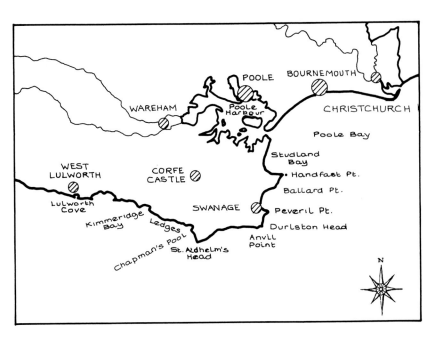

relief at having escaped a watery grave soon turned to terror when faced with a cutlass-waving crowd of locals who threatened to 'make the ship a wreck' if they dared to protest at the plunder.

For hundreds of years the 'barbarous plundering' of wrecked vessels continued unabated. By 1713 it had become so serious that an Act of Parliament was passed 'to better protect the fate of vessels in distress and their cargoes'. Among its provisions it required clergymen in coastal parishes to read the Act to their congregations 'four times in the Year in all the Parish Churches and Chapels of every Sea Port Town', reminding their errant flocks of the penalties which could be incurred if they stole goods from ships cast ashore. The advice appears to have had little effect in Dorset, some of the worst instances of looting occurring late in the eighteenth century. Indeed, the author of a shipwreck account published in 1796 accused the priest in one of the Chesil villages of positively encouraging the 'cruel rapacity' of his parishioners as they eagerly anticipated the wrecks of vessels on Chesil Beach.

The turn of the century was to bring a gradual lessening of such violent scenes, and in the 1800's saving of life at last began to take priority over the pillaging of cargoes. Once all those who could be rescued had been brought to safety, the removal of any goods on board continued to be considered 'fair reward' for many years. The chance of taking away some choice items of cargo remained a more appealing and often more profitable alternative to submitting a legitimate salvage claim!

Ships in the days of sail found the Dorset coastline almost as inhospitable as its inhabitants. In its centre, thrust out into the Channel, is the Island of Portland. Portland Bill and its lighthouse are both landmark and warning to those who stray too near its rocky shores. Just to the south east lies the Shambles Sandbank, only ten feet or so below the surface at low tide. Lying in wait at the Bill is the notorious Portland Race, a cauldron of turbulent tidal waters eager to engulf any vessel unlucky or unwary enough to venture too close.

To the west of Portland there is little in the way of a safe anchorage until Lyme Regis is reached, a distance of some twenty five miles. Bridport's Harbour (now known as West Bay) is a man-made cutting through Chesil Beach, dangerous to enter in rough weather and one which the sea constantly seeks to destroy. Even Lyme's stone Cobb, first constructed in mediaeval times to provide a haven for shipping, has been breached and rebuilt on several occasions.

Between Portland and Bridport lies that most dangerous of lee shores, Chesil Beach. Countless vessels caught in south westerly gales and trapped in the West Bay have been ensnared by this extraordinary arc of steeply shelving shingle. Eighteen miles of stones which are curiously and meticulously sorted by the sea, the fine gravel at its western end gradually increasing in size along the length of the beach until the pebbles are fist-sized at Portland. Wily smugglers, it is said, could tell where they had landed in the blackness of the night simply by grasping a handful of stones and judging their size. At Chesil's Portland end lies Deadman's Bay, legendary graveyard of ships and sailors driven onto this unforgiving shore.

'And once on the beach, the sea has little mercy, for the water is deep right in, and the waves curl over and fall on the pebbles with a weight no timbers can withstand. Then if the poor fellows try to save themselves, there is a deadly undertow or rush back of the water,

Lighthouses were first built at Portland Bill in 1716. This fine atmospheric photograph of the 1869 old Lower Lighthouse was taken in about 1900: it has now been converted to a bird observatory. The present lighthouse came into use in 1906.

Three light vessels have warned of the dangers of the submerged shingle bank off Portland since the first *Shambles Lightship* was stationed here in 1859. This is the second (1883-1947). The third was replaced by an automatic buoy in 1973.

which sucks them off their legs, and carries them again under the thundering waves'. So wrote John Meade Falkner in *Moonfleet*, the classic adventure story of the Dorset coast.

Behind Chesil, between Wyke and Abbotsbury, lie the brackish waters of The Fleet. Remote and quiet now, but in times gone by The Fleet saw scenes of feverish activity when a ship came ashore on Chesil Beach. On stormy nights small boats were ready to cross from the mainland as their owners chanted with glee: 'Blow wind, rise storm. Ship ashore before morn.'

Chesil Beach was less menacing to those seeking shelter on the east side of Portland. Here it forms a protective arm between the Island and the mainland and shelters Portland Roads. These waters were a safe haven for shipping long before the Victorian breakwaters were built to enclose Portland Harbour. Beyond Weymouth's harbour and its calm bay the coastline changes again to the miles of steep cliffs, stony beaches and treacherous rocky underwater ledges which lead to Purbeck. Before the vast harbour of Poole is reached, there are the tricky headlands of St Aldhelm's (sometimes St Alban's), Durlston – the site of Dorset's second lighthouse at Anvil Point, and Peveril and Handfast Points.

The sea has shaped Dorset's history and shipwrecks are inevitably a part of that history. Shipwreck stories have their heroes and their villains. For all the lurid tales of violence and looting there are accounts in equal numbers of heroic rescues against all the odds. Time and time again, Dorset folk who know and understand the sea have risked their lives to save those in peril on it.

PLUNDER

The practice of wrecking, or plundering, the cargoes of shipwrecked vessels dates back many centuries. As early as 1305 over 200 local people were named as the plunderers of a Spanish ship driven ashore in a gale near Portland, and in 1322 a Devon merchant accused pirates from the Weymouth and Portland neighbourhood of attacking one of his ships and driving her into Lyme, where they boarded, ransacked and scuttled her.

In 1641 the *Golden Grape* was forced on Chesil Beach near Wyke Regis 'by an extremity of fowle weather'. Seven of her crew of twenty were drowned and soon hundreds of locals were on the beach looting her cargo. On a voyage from Cadiz to Dover the ship was laden with 2000 barrels of raisins, 400 jars of oil, 12 butts of wine, fruit, silk, silver plate and bullion and gold and silver coins. Boats were soon plying across The Fleet taking the plunderers and their booty back to the mainland for a fee, usually a share of the stolen cargo. In evidence given later the master of the *Golden Grape* spoke of the 'force and violence' by which his vessel had been robbed by the country people.

When the *Katherine* of Brest was lost at Portland in 1702, the Customs officers who tried to supervise the salvage of her contents complained that not only had the locals carried away the cargo of chestnuts, they had also 'beat and abus'd ye officers in ye execution of their Dutyes'.

The wildest scenes of looting occurred in 1749 when the *Hope* foundered on Chesil Beach. The loss of the Dutch vessel bears all the hallmarks of a riproaring adventure yarn: a dark and stormy night, a 'pirate' ship laden with gold, wrecked, perhaps deliberately, and plundered on a vast scale by a violent mob . . .

The *Hope* had been away from her home port, Amsterdam, for many months on a most profitable expedition. Laden with a good mixed cargo, Captain Booy Cornelisz had taken his ship first to Curacao, a Dutch possession in the·West Indies. He then sailed for the Spanish Main, the northernmost part of South America, where Spanish colonists were exploiting the gold and silver mines and plantations of the New World. Spain watched over her overseas possessions jealously. Foreign traders were not welcome and the Dutch *Hope* was armed with 30 guns to repel any attempt at capture by Spanish guard ships. The Spanish settlers themselves were happy to trade with whoever came their way. They saw few ships from their own country, wanted to buy European goods and had gold and silver in plenty to pay for them. The *Hope* was, in effect, involved in smuggling, an illegal and dangerous trade with high rewards. When she sailed for home Cornelisz's so-called 'pirate' ship was reputed to be carrying £50,000 in gold, silver and coin.

Nearing the end of this long voyage, the *Hope* encountered bad weather in the English Channel and on 16 January 1749, storms tossed her on Chesil Beach almost opposite Fleet House. Is there a suggestion of deliberate wrecking in the accounts of that night? One writer claimed that no light appeared from the lighthouses in Portland: 'whether from intense mists and particular fogginess of the air, or from the neglects of the persons concern'd, I shall not pretend to determine'.

Few ships survive long on the shingle beach and it was fortunate that the *Hope*'s masts fell across the pebbles, enabling her crew to scramble to safety. In the darkness the men could only wait, listening to the waves hurling stones down on their ship as it broke up. Daylight brought the looters, well-armed with knives, clubs and hooks. 'These people', wrote the author of an account of the wreck published in its wake, '. . .came not with the dispositions of men, but those.of beasts of prey; they came for rapine and plunder.'

The 'merciless battalion' was commanded by Augustin Elliott of Portland, later accused of being 'the muster master, treasurer and divider of prey among his plundering regiment'. He organised his men well, and parties of twenty systematically searched the beach and collected up any goods that floated ashore. The theft of the cargo continued for well over a week and to get off the beach with a few of their salvaged goods, Cornelisz and his men had to haul their

An AUTHENTICK

ACCOUNT

OF THE

HOPE,

A VERY RICH

DUTCH Merchant-Ship

Laden with Money and Goods,

THAT WAS

Caſt-away on PORTLAND-BEACH

IN THE

County of *D O R S E T,*

The 16th of *January,* 1748.

WITH THE

Manner of her being plunder'd by a vaſt Con-
courſe of PEOPLE.

AND THE

Trial at large of *A. Elliott,* who was tried at the Aſ-
ſizes held at *Dorcheſter* the 15th of *July,* 1749;
for feloniouſly carrying away Part of her Cargoe.

By a GENTLEMAN in the Neighbourhood

Accounts of notable shipwrecks were popular and often ran to several
editions. In dating the wreck of the *Hope* to 1748, the author has used the
old-style calendar. From 1752 the New Year officially commenced on
January 1st and the old usage of Lady Day, 25th March, as the
start of the year was dropped.

own boat down the shingle to cross The Fleet. The *Hope* was the richest ship ever to be wrecked on Chesil and as tales of her value spread, so the size of the mob increased from hundreds to thousands, all turning over the stones in the raw January weather, determined not to leave without a handful of gold. Eventually Captain Lisle of the Weymouth Customs arrived armed and with 30 men. Unable to control the situation, he called for reinforcements and when 130 more men arrived, Lisle was able to take charge and begin organizing the proper salvage of what remained.

There is no real explanation of why it took so long to disperse the mob. The Portland Excise Officer had visited the scene twice and was severely criticised for taking no action, but the sight of 2000 people, many of them his neighbours, armed and searching for treasure may have quite easily persuaded him that it was prudent to turn a blind eye. There were rumours that looters died fighting over the booty and early reports stated that two of the Dutch crew had drawn knives and killed each other in an argument over what little of the ship's cargo they had saved for themselves.

Augustin Elliott was charged at Dorchester Assizes in July 1749 with 'feloniously carrying away part of the *Hope*'s cargo'. By this time most of the Dutchmen had returned home and only the Captain and First Mate remained. All the local people who had been at the scene claimed Elliott was innocent of any wrongdoing and that he was in favour of returning the cargo to its rightful owners.

What had actually happened was that on 24 January the looters had gathered at a public house in the village of Chesil, clamouring for Elliott to share out the booty, which he did at £7 per head. Much of the money was later returned, but, as the prosecution pointed out, not until four days after Elliott was committed for trial, possibly only then in the hope of mitigating the charge against him.

Despite overwhelming evidence against them, Elliott and three others tried for similar offences were all found 'Not Guilty'. The final paragraph of the account of the trial is the most telling: 'As at a moderate computation, 10,000 from all Parts of this county, of farmers, tradesmen, labourers, with one L--d of a M---r, have been concern'd either in the carrying away Part of the Property of this ship themselves, or in purchasing the same from them that did so: it is therefore far from being any matter of wonder to find the j--y under a strong disposition to favour such as were tried for offences of this kind'.

The judge remarked that he hoped the proceedings might have had their proper design and influence 'in causing of crimes of this sort to cease amongst us'.

Not long afterwards a French vessel drove on Chesil Beach and the 2000 people who arrived on the scene carried off 'every Thing they could lay their Hands on'. Customs officers were told they would be 'cut down with their Hatchets or thrown into the Sea' if they interfered. 'These are', continues the report, 'the very same Fellows who plunder'd and broke up the Dutch Ship that was on shore about six months ago near the same Place'.

Five years later the congregations in the Chesil churches received rather more than the customary statutory reminder about the illegality of removing the cargoes of wrecked ships. Thomas Francklyn, Rector of Langton Herring and Vicar of Fleet, preached a sermon which he addressed 'particularly to those in the neighbourhood of Weymouth and Portland' and his stern words were later published under the title *Serious advice and Fair Warning to all that live upon the sea-coast of England and Wales*, with an appendix setting out the penalties which could be incurred by those who were apprehended.

The sermon had little lasting effect. In 1762 the locals robbed the crew of a wrecked French ship and stripped them of their clothes, and in 1795 the battered and bruised survivors of the ships of Admiral Christian's fleet were callously disregarded as they pleaded for assistance on Chesil Beach.

1795 saw the French threatening British supremacy in the West Indies. Reinforcements were required and a large fleet of some 200 heavily-laden troop and ordnance transports and merchant ships put to sea from Spithead on 15 November 1795. They were under the command of Rear Admiral Hugh Cloberry Christian. Proceeding slowly down the Channel the West Indies-bound ships were a fine sight and spectators gathered on vantage points along the coast to view them. Within two days of setting sail the fleet was in trouble. Severe south westerly gales sprang up and Christian gave the order that they should make for Torbay. It was a poor decision. Some of his ships were already close to the dangers of Portland and the Chesil Beach. When a second order commanded them to stand out to sea it was too late. At daybreak on the 18th six vessels were flung on the shingle bank. Two ordnance transports were lost between Wyke Regis and Portland. The *Aeolus*, 153-tons, struck first, followed by a larger vessel, the *Golden Grove*. To the west, on the beach opposite Fleet and Chickerell, three troop transports, the *Piedmont*, *Catherine* and *Venus* and a merchantman, the *Thomas*, were quickly smashed to pieces. The full horror of these shipwrecks is described in an eyewitness account in a local newspaper of 26 November 1795:

'The shore from hence (Weymouth) to Abbotsbury, about seven miles distant, is still covered with dead bodies, and parts of the wrecks hourly thrown up. I yesterday counted nine dead bodies thrown upon the beach by one tide, within the space of quarter of a mile ... Part of the Gloucester Militia, aided by the peasantry are constantly employed in burying them. The number of sufferers almost exceeds belief: upwards of 1600 bodies, having, it is said, been thrown up along the beach. An officer of the Gloucester Militia has told me he assisted at the burial of 300'.

Early estimates of the number drowned were exaggerated and the total was probably around 300, but it was a most dreadful scene: 'the Chesil Bank was strewn for about two miles with the dead bodies of men and animals, with pieces of wreck, and piles of plundered goods, which groups of people were at work to carry away, regardless of the sight of the drowned bodies that filled the newly arrived spectators with grief and amazement'.

So intent were the looters in getting their stolen goods back to the mainland that shipwreck victims had difficulty finding places on the busy ferry boats which plied across The Fleet, rowed by those who 'neglected to give the wretched sufferers the smallest assistance'. Mass graves had to be dug on the landward side of Chesil. Consecrated ground was not a requirement for burials in the eighteenth century and it was not uncommon to bury shipwreck victims where they were found. This was the last resting place of the ordinary soldiers and sailors, the spot once marked by piles of stones, now long gone. Women were interred in the churchyard at Wyke Regis, as were officers who could be identified. Many of the bodies had been bruised and disfigured beyond recognition by the force of the sea. Hands were examined to establish rank – if they were cared for and obviously unaccustomed to hard labour, the body was judged to be that of an officer.

A young woman was one of only two survivors from the troop transport *Catherine* and she was left destitute by the tragedy which drowned her husband and forty others on board. He was Cornet William Stukely Burns of the 26th Light Dragoons, an American whose allegiance to the British flag had led to his disinheritance by his family. His widow's first-hand account of her awful experience on Chesil Beach was used by Charlotte Smith, a popular literary figure of the time, in her '*Narrative. . .*' of the wrecks of Admiral Christian's Fleet. It was sold 'for the Benefit of an unfortunate Survivor from one of the Wrecks, and her Infant Child' and raised funds for

The *Catherine*, lost on Chesil Beach, 1795. One passenger who later drowned in the wreck was sadly mistaken when he observed that 'there was a good shore near and all would do well.' One of the two survivors of the forty on board, Mrs Burns, is visible below the quarterdeck.

Mrs Burns who stayed on in Weymouth and raised her son in the town. Although their pleas for help had been virtually ignored on the beach, once on the mainland survivors were more humanely treated and most did then receive care and medical attention.

The rest of the ill-fated fleet made its way back to Spithead and reassembled. A number of ships had sought shelter in Weymouth Bay, including the dismasted *Hope* and *Firm*. The *Hannah* had stranded east of Weymouth and the *Pitt* went ashore at St Aldhelm's Head, both without casualties. The Admiral survived the gales and returned in his damaged flagship *Prince George*. Transferring his flag to the *Glory* he again set sail with his fleet on 9 December, only to be forced back a second time when gales scattered his ships in the Bay of Biscay. Admiral Christian eventually reached Barbados in April 1796.

THE EAST INDIAMEN

'East Indiamen' were the aristocrats of the maritime world. The magnificent, showy ships of the English East India Company made long hazardous voyages to bring home exotic goods from the other side of the globe. In the eighteenth and early nineteenth centuries they left London bound for India and China, sailing down the Channel well-laden with cargo to sell out East. They returned filled with fashionable fabrics – chintz, muslin and silks; porcelain, carvings and Oriental *objets d'art*; and quantities of that most fashionable drink tea, from Canton.

Three of these prestigious ships were lost on Dorset's coast. Two were outward bound and had been at sea only days – the *Halsewell*, wrecked below Worth Matravers in 1786, and the *Earl of Abergavenny*, lost off Weymouth in 1805. A third ship, the *Alexander*, was almost safely home from Bengal when she foundered on Chesil Beach in 1815.

'Never did happen so complete a wreck', wrote vicar Morgan Jones in Worth Matravers parish register following the loss of the *Halsewell* in January 1786. The 758-ton ship struck the rocks just east of St Aldhelm's Head in appalling weather conditions. She had left London for Bengal on New Year's Day and encountered gales with heavy snowfalls on only the second day of her voyage. It was the beginning of an agonizing struggle for survival. In an attempt to wear the ship and stay afloat, first her mizen mast and then her main mast were cut down – a dangerous manoeuvre during which five men were swept overboard and drowned. Leaking badly and apparently not much aided by some of the crew 'who had skulked in their hammocks during the storm', the ship endeavoured to weather Peveril Point and reach the shelter of Studland Bay, but it proved an impossible goal. The day before the ship struck, even her chief officer observed that there was very little hope. Distress guns were fired but they went unheard in the violence of the gale. The *Halsewell* was thrown on the rocks below Seacombe Cliffs in the early hours of Friday, 6 January.

It was a desperate situation. The *Halsewell* came in broadside on under the overhanging ledge of a cave. Little of the tragedy was visible from the clifftop, which in any case was so sparsely populated that rescue was unlikely. Holed already, the ship was soon torn apart by violent seas and much of the wreckage sank from view very quickly. Those who managed to struggle onto the rocks in the darkness had little to cling to and 200 feet of sheer cliff above them. Many lost their hold in the wet, freezing conditions and slipped into the sea to join those who had already drowned in the wreck. Only at daybreak, when two of the crew successfully scaled the cliffs to raise the alarm were ropes brought by Purbeck quarrymen who hauled the survivors to safety. Even some of these lost their grip during the

A contemporary account described the spot where the *Halsewell* was wrecked in 1786 : 'But at this particular spot the cliff is excavated at the foot and presents a cavern of ten or twelve yards in depth, and of breadth equal to the length of a large ship . . . It was at the mouth of this cavern that the unfortunate wreck lay stretched almost from side to side of it, and offering her broadside to the horrid chasm.'

'Captain Pierce, a little while before the ship went down, called Mr Meriton into the cuddy, where his two daughters, two nieces and three other beautiful young ladies were clinging round him for protection . . .' All were lost in the 1786 wreck of the *Halsewell*.

perilous ascent and fell to their deaths on the rocks below. There is no accurate listing of all those who were on board the *Halsewell*. Although more than 70 were saved it was certainly less than a third of those who sailed in her – some 160 lost their lives.

An eyewitness described the scene that morning: 'In the different recesses of the rocks a confused heap of boards, broken masts, chests, trunks and dead bodies were all huddled together, and the face of the water as far as the eye could extend was disfigured with floating carcasses, tables, chairs, casks and part of every other article in the vessel'.

The commander of the *Halsewell* drowned in the wreck, leaving behind him a widow and six children. Captain Richard Pierce had intended this to be his final voyage before retirement. He was wealthy, for there were many fringe benefits for a man in his position, 'private trading' being the most profitable. Captains were allowed to take their own cargo to sell out East, quite separate from that of the East India Company. Pierce was estimated to have made 'a competent fortune' from his previous voyages. In his charge were seven young women, most, it would seem, leaving England to be the brides of wealthy gentlemen overseas. Two were his own daughters, seventeen-year-old Eliza and Mary Anne, aged fifteen, and two his nieces. This emigration of girls destined for marriage abroad seems to have been an accepted, if not wholly approved of, feature of these voyages: ' . . . beautiful young women are now reckoned among the articles of our export trade to India. Not one ship is sailing without a cargo on board and they are literally going to market . . . '

The *Earl of Abergavenny*, 1200-tons, left Gravesend at the end of January 1805, bound for Bengal and China. She was under the command of Captain John Wordsworth, brother of the Poet Laureate, William, and reached Portsmouth safely, despite a collision with another vessel in the Downs. On her fifth voyage, she was,

The East Indiaman *Earl of Abergavenny*. Oil painting by Thomas Luny, 1801.

according to her master, 'the finest ship in the fleet', and said by the East India Company to be 'the favourite ship of the season', an indication that she offered the least discomfort in an age when long voyages were notoriously cramped and unpleasant.

Shortly after the *Earl of Abergavenny* left Portsmouth in convoy, the unpredictable Channel weather worsened; the ships were ordered to put into Portland Roads, and Wordsworth awaited the arrival of a pilot. An hour after he had been taken on board, the East Indiaman struck The Shambles sandbank where she stuck fast. It is said that Wordsworth's words were 'O Pilot, pilot, you have ruined me!' and accounts of the wreck do indeed note that the pilot 'did not seem well acquainted with the coast', a curious statement with regard to one whose local skills had been employed to negotiate its hazards.

The *Earl of Abergavenny* was aground for some hours. The seriousness of the situation was not immediately realised and although a boat left the scene to summon assistance, a boat which came out from the shore took off only a few passengers. In the evening the badly-holed East Indiaman floated free. Wordsworth hoped to make a run for Weymouth Sands, but his waterlogged ship began to drift, the pumps unable to cope. Local boats which came out could not or would not approach close enough to rescue those on board.

At 11 pm on Tuesday, 5 February 1805, the *Earl of Abergavenny* sank in shallow water. She was less than two miles off Weymouth Esplanade, her masts and rigging above the waves. Numbers of her crew and passengers clung to the shrouds and some were saved. Many more tumbled into the sea in the freezing conditions and were drowned. Captain Wordsworth died with his ship, as did some 260 other souls, almost two thirds of the 400 who had set out on that fateful voyage.

Several accounts were published following the wreck, all claiming to be 'true' and 'authentic' but differing in detail regarding the sequence of events. Certainly Wordsworth was not aware of the extent of the damage to his vessel, since his initial plan once he got her off The Shambles was to run for Portsmouth. His sailors did appreciate the futility of trying to pump out the sea water which was steadily flooding the ship. They demanded entrance to the spirits room, reasoning that if they were going down they might just as well

'A few appear at morning light
Preserved upon the tall mast's height . . .'
Two lines from William Wordsworth's poem describing the loss of the *Earl of Abergavenny* in 1805 and the death of his brother, John.

be drunk as sober. There were delays in rescuing those who clung to the rigging and there were suggestions that the local boats might be hoping to pick up cargo rather than survivors. It had certainly been a 'most melancholy event'.

The masts of the sunken ship remained visible for many months. Abigail Gawthern, a summer-season visitor to Weymouth in 1805, wrote in her diary: 'walked a little on the Esplanade, saw the masts of the *Abergavenny*, a most melancholy sight; I rejoice I do not see them from my lodgings'.

The ship was valuable, heavily laden with cargo said to contain, '£67,000 value in Dollars, packed in 62 chests, Copper, Tin, Lead and Iron, 200-tons each . . . Cloth, Haberdashery, Millinery, Glass, Wedgwood Ware, Harness, Saddles, Military Stores, Wines . . . etc.'

It was also all underwater, so there was no chance of the locals carrying out their usual plundering raids. Salvage contractor John

John Braithwaite and his divers on the *Endeavour* worked on the
Earl of Abergavenny for many months – ' . . . till the cargo got so
thin, not worth getting up'.

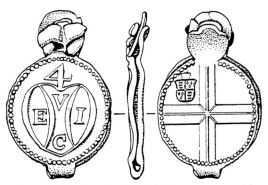

Recent finds from the *Earl of Abergavenny* wreck
site include lead cloth seals such as these, bearing
the insignia of the East India Company.
Drawn by Hazel Martingell.

Braithwaite was called in to work on the wreck. He and his men on the *Endeavour* began diving operations in February 1806 and over the following months successfully brought to the surface vast quantities of linen, silk, muslin, ribbons, gloves, great coats, silk handkerchiefs, boots, perfumery, glassware and a host of other items, including the most valuable part of the cargo, the 62 chests of dollars estimated to be worth some £12,000 apiece.

One intrepid lady visitor's holiday in Weymouth that summer was considerably enlivened by a trip beneath the waves in Mr Braithwaite's diving bell. Following her safe return from the forty minute descent, the local press, predictably, could not resist nicknaming Mrs Bennett 'the diving belle'.

Braithwaite used gunpowder on several occasions to break open the ship and reveal more of her cargo. It was used again to give the ship 'a gentle shake' when the Deane brothers carried out further salvage work in the 1840s, and in 1921 the Navy blew up the *Earl of Abergavenny* as she was considered to be a hazard to shipping. Despite being thus scattered on the sea bed the East Indiaman remains a site of great interest even today, and a diving team led by Ed Cumming has produced detailed drawings of the ship and its artefacts.

The third of Dorset's lost East Indiamen was the *Alexander*, wrecked on Chesil Beach in 1815. By this date the English East India Company had lost its monopoly of the trading route to India. The *Alexander* was owned by the prominent trading firm of Charles Forbes and Co. Tragically near the end of a voyage which had begun in Bombay in October 1814, she was thrown onto the beach opposite the passage house at Wyke during a violent gale on Easter Monday, 27 March 1815. It is likely that no-one saw or heard the ship come ashore in the early hours and only five survived out of her complement of 150 crew and passengers: 'she struck at 2 a.m. and at four she was a complete wreck, and every soul on board were consigned to a watery grave, excepting four Malays and one Persian'.

Chesil next morning was strewn with bodies and wreckage from Abbotsbury to Portland. None of the five crew who survived spoke any English, so the exact circumstances of the wreck are unknown. But it can be assumed that her passengers were people of some standing, for there are two memorials to those who lost their lives on the *Alexander* at Wyke Regis Church. A gravestone in the churchyard was erected by the owners of the ship – its words now indecipherable. The second memorial is a prominent carved stone on the outside wall of the church – a particularly fine monument which was designed by Weymouth's best-known Georgian architect, James Hamilton.

Oddly enough, it is the *Alexander*, the least known of Dorset's wrecked East Indiamen which has the most lasting local memorials. The *Earl of Abergavenny*'s Captain John Wordsworth lies in an unmarked grave in the same churchyard, others who died in his ship are buried here or at Radipole Church. William Wordsworth was much distressed by his brother's death and the following lines are taken from the 'Elegiac Verses' he wrote after the tragedy:

> *All vanished in a single word,*
> *A breath, a sound, and scarcely heard.*
> *Sea – Ship – drowned – Shipwreck – so it came,*
> *The meek, the brave, the good, was gone:*
> *He who had been our living John*
> *Was nothing but a name.*

The victims of the *Halsewell* tragedy were interred close to where they were found, the exact location now unknown, at Seacombe Bottom, a lonely spot. There are literary links here, too. When King George III visited the disaster site during his first visit to Weymouth in 1789, three years after the wreck, local poet William Holloway commemorated the occasion in verse. In 1853, Charles Dickens published 'The Long Voyage' in his weekly periodical 'Household Words'. It was a collection of sea stories remembered from his childhood, one of which was the account of the loss of the *Halsewell*.

THE GALES
1824 AND 1838

Those who lived in Dorset's coastal towns and villages were well-used to the fierce gales which threw up on their shores wrecked ships, spilled cargoes and drowned men. Nothing, though, prepared them for the terrifying night of 22/23 November 1824, when a storm which had been blowing all day rose in the darkness of the early hours to become a destructive hurricane of such violence that it has gone down in history as the 'Great Gale'. One eye-witness was the Rector of Wyke Regis, George Chamberlaine, who recorded its passing at the end of the Register of Baptisms: 'Tuesday 23 November 1824 – it blew a most dreadful Hurricane, such as never had been known before in the memory of Man'.

The gale ripped across the whole of south-west England and left a trail of devastation in its wake. Howling winds ripped off roofs and chimneys and tore down whole buildings. Trees by the thousand were uprooted, hayricks scattered and cows and sheep drowned as rivers overflowed. Along the coast, already high spring tides rose to unheard of heights and brought misery and destruction. Huge waves swept away piers and quays. Sea walls were breached. Wrecked ships littered the coasts of Hampshire, Dorset, Devon and Cornwall.

At Portland, giant seas swept over Chesil Beach and crashed down on the village of Chesil, demolishing more than thirty houses and so damaging a hundred others that they were uninhabitable. Twenty five Portlanders drowned in the deluge, some buried under their homes, others swept away by the sea. The ferry between the Island and mainland was washed away, as were boats and nets (and livelihoods) of the local fishermen. In the days that followed it was not only their own dead that the Islanders were burying; each tide threw up on the beach the bodies of those lost at sea.

Seventeen were from the West Indiaman *Colville*, outward bound from London. One of her passengers, realising his fate as the ship drove on Chesil Beach, had the remarkable presence of mind to tear off a piece of his shirt, on which he wrote his name and address before tying it around his neck. Henry Gosling's body was thus identified in an age when many hundreds of shipwreck victims had to be anonymously buried. Off Portland, in that terrible storm 'a large vessel of 500-tons burthen, name unknown, went down and the whole crew perished'.

Most of those on board the *Ebenezer* were more fortunate. Carrying government stores from Plymouth to Portsmouth, the 80-ton vessel was flung very high on Chesil Beach, so high in fact, that it proved easier to haul her up to the top of the beach and down the shingle on the opposite side when the time came to relaunch her after repairs. Although her captain lost his life in the gale, the rest of the crew were saved.

At Fleet, enormous seas practically engulfed the tiny village, knocking down its church and several cottages. Here, the *Carvalho*, laden with rum and cotton, was lost with all hands. A little to the west a Danish brig, carrying a cargo of fruit, was driven ashore. Four of her five-man crew were rescued.

Weymouth residents awoke to find the pier much damaged by the force of the sea, which had also demolished most of the Esplanade. Basements of the fine seafront terraces were filled with sand and water and boats swept from their moorings were floating down the town's main streets. At a place called 'The Narrows', sea and backwater joined across the roadway and swept a man to his death.

Two smacks were lost, the *Louisa* of Exeter and the *Sally* of Portsmouth. The master of the former was rescued, but two crew drowned. The only survivor from the *Sally* saved himself by jumping onto the Weymouth brig *Nancy* as the two vessels smashed together. Dismasted and damaged, the *Nancy* rode out the gale. Near Sandsfoot Castle a Dutch galliott, the *Johanna Christina*, broke from her moorings and drove ashore.

At Lyme Regis there was excitement and alarm as onlookers who watched giant waves breaking over the newly-extended Cobb saw it give way under the pounding. A great surge of water swept across the

The wreck of the *Unity* at Lyme Regis in 1824. '. . . the mothers, wives, sisters and friends of the crew joined in the general rush towards the Church Cliffs, crying and screaming in agonies to see the poor fellows in the shrouds.'

harbour, tearing a local fishing smack from her moorings. The Lyme-built trawler *Caroline* was next, driven to the river-mouth where she was wrecked by tremendous breakers. The plight of those on board the local Revenue Cruiser *Fox* caused great distress. As she drifted, damaged and helpless, two men on board who attempted to swim for their lives were drowned. One left a widow and six children, and five children were left fatherless by the death of the other. The *Mary and Elizabeth*, laden with sailcloth and bound for Guernsey, had three times returned to Lyme for shelter due to bad weather and now had the misfortune to be blown ashore. The *Unity* was the next casualty. Fully laden, with her captain and crew on board, the London trader was driven under the cliffs between Lyme and Charmouth where a daring rescue, co-ordinated by Captain C.C. Bennett, RN, brought all her crew to safety. News was also to reach Lyme of the loss of one of the town's schooners off the Cornish coast. In the wreck of Mr James Kerridge's *Happy Return*, he and the entire crew except one lad had been drowned.

The bad weather continued, as did the reports of shipping

Lost on Chesil Beach in the 1838 gales was 'the sloop
Dove of Weymouth, Captain Bussell, happily all
hands were saved, and also part of the cargo'.

casualties. A week after the Great Gale yet another tragedy was
played out on Chesil Beach when the Dutch galliott *Leonora* drove
ashore between Wyke and Portland. Her crew and cargo shared the
same fate: 'Nothing whatever has been saved'.

The second of Dorset's infamous nineteenth century storms took
place in 1838. Strong autumnal winds had been blowing for several
days, when on the afternoon of Wednesday, November 28 they
finally reached gale force. Twenty-four hours later wrecked vessels
were scattered all along the Dorset coast.

'Something like an estimate of the devastation of the storm may be
gathered from the circumstances that the coast between Lyme and
St Alban's Head presents the wrecks of no less than seventeen or
eighteen vessels, many of which have been dashed to pieces without a
soul having been saved.' (Extract from the *Dorset County Chronicle*,
6 December 1838)

First ashore on Chesil was a 70-ton Weymouth sloop, the *Dove*.
With local knowledge of the deadly West Bay, Captain Bussell saw
the futility of trying to save the vessel and he and his crew

abandoned ship safely before she struck. The Africa-bound schooner *Columbine* foundered next, a total loss with all on board. Her passengers included two Wesleyan missionaries who were later buried in the Methodist graveyard at Fortuneswell. All were saved when the Swedish barque *Louise* was swept on the beach. To the west, off Fleet, the *Arethusa*, bound for Antigua, went down with all hands and at Abbotsbury only one was rescued from the *Mary Ann*, a Plymouth schooner.

Chesil Beach claimed yet more lives in these gales. Portlander William Pearce of the Coastguard Service was on duty beside several of the wrecked vessels and died when he was struck by lightning. Three local men were drowned at Chickerell as they tried to cross The Fleet in a small boat.

Just north of Weymouth, Bowleaze was the scene of a dramatic rescue when a French brig went on shore. The *Marie Louise* had five on board. Her captain and two others were rescued with some difficulty but there seemed little hope for two lads left on the vessel. Local coastguard John Mantle swam out through raging seas and eventually managed to bring both to safety. As well as being awarded lifesaving medals for his bravery that night, Coastguard Mantle was presented with a watch from the Mayor and citizens of Weymouth and a gold medal from the French Government.

Not all those on board another French vessel were so fortunate, despite the sterling efforts made to save them at Bridport. *Le Jean Bart*, a smack carrying hides, drifted under the 200 feet high cliffs east of the harbour entrance. Despite dreadful conditions local rescuers managed to haul five of those on board to the top of the cliff. Sadly, one other fell to his death when sharp rocks severed the rope, a passenger could not be persuaded to leave the wreck and *Le Jean Bart*'s captain, who had remained at the foot of the cliff to assist in the rescue, became exhausted and heavy seas washed him away.

Along the Purbeck coast 'pieces of wreck, casks of wine, spars and cordage', many from unidentified vessels, were continually driving on shore. Casks of wine from the *Joseph Desiri* littered Worbarrow Bay, many shattered and some, regrettably, mixed with salt water! All eight on board the French *châsse marée* had been saved by the Kimmeridge Coastguards.

This 'shipwreck souvenir' is labelled 'A present from Weymouth, made from the *Columbine* wrecked on Portland Beach November 28th 1838'. It was sold at Medhurst's Tunbridge Ware Manufactory, Chesterfield Place, Esplanade, Weymouth.

Although the inevitable plundering followed the wrecks, the local press reported that, 'It is gratifying to be able to state that the people of Portland and of many places lying on the West Bay behaved in a manner becoming to humanity and exerted themselves at imminent peril to save the life and property of others. It is, notwithstanding, lamentable to have to record that there were exceptions to this general good behaviour, and an examination yesterday took place at the County Hall in this town, before the magistrates, when eleven persons of the neighbourhood of Abbotsbury were committed for further examination on charges of plundering from wrecks and bodies cast ashore on that part of the coast'.

SAIL AND STEAM
1800 – 1900

A new type of vessel was to appear in the shipping casualty lists of the first half of the nineteenth century – the steamship. Probably the first known wreck of a steamer on the Dorset coast was that of the Channel Islands Post Office Packet *Meteor*, lost at Portland on 23 February 1830. The paddler went aground in hazy, but not severe weather conditions at Church Ope Cove (the reality was very different to the dramatic storm shown in the print on the opposite page). Rescuers got everyone off safely.

After this incident Dorset's steamship losses were for some years few and far between, but later in the century their numbers increased. Sailing vessels continued to founder almost routinely, causing little comment in the local newspapers. In these small weekly publications much column space was devoted to national and foreign news; local events, if reported at all, were often confined to a few lines. Typically brief is the *Sherborne Mercury*'s account of a shipwreck in January 1807: 'On Friday the 9th inst. a Swedish galliot called the *Johanna Elizabeth*, laden with brandy, wine and salt, etc. was wrecked on Abbotsbury Bay; two men were drowned, and five men and a boy were saved'

There were many others: July 1802 – the *Betsey*, laden with stone, lost as she lay at anchor in Studland Bay; January 1817 (during another of Dorset's severe storms when vessels foundered all along the coast) – the Portsmouth sloop *Sarah*, driven on shore at Lulworth Cove, all hands saved; March 1821 – a French brig, *Arthur Le Juvenale*, a total loss on Langton Beach, all saved except one boy, its cargo of coffee and cotton totally lost; January 1823 – a smugglers' boat, the *Mary* of Cowes, attempting to land her cargo of spirits, capsized and the whole crew drowned, eight casks seized by the

Loss of the Steam Packet *Meteor*, 1830. 'The profits arising from the sale of these Prints will be divided among the CREW for their great exertions in saving the lives of all the Passengers on board by ropes on the principle of Captn. Manby's Apparatus; most of the baggage was also landed but the greatest part carried off or destroyed by the Inhabitants of the Island'.

Preventive Men and taken to His Majesty's warehouse at Poole; December 1830 – a French *châsse marée* on shore at the south-east part of Portland, totally wrecked, two of the crew were saved, the master and a boy drowned . . .

In raging seas establishing contact with a vessel offshore was both difficult and dangerous. Portland once had its own 'rescue dogs', trained from puppyhood to swim in almost any sea. Collectors of smuggled goods and flotsam and jetsam, they also took out ropes to ships in distress – as is described in this extract from an early nineteenth century poem.

> For Portland had a name both far and wide
> For dogs well trained and of a noble breed;
> 'Twas theirs to stem the dangers of the tide,
> To bear a rope to seamen in their need
> Which fastened to the barque by vigorous hand
> The brave imperilled crew might reach the land.

Ropes thrown from shore to ship became sodden and heavy, and in the early 1800s Norfolk inventor Captain George Manby designed a portable carriage carrying a mortar which *fired* a line on board with some accuracy. The use of the Manby Lifesaving Apparatus was soon widespread, its mortars replaced by rockets later in the century. There were very few regular lifeboat services and those which did exist were locally run. Rescue operations were the responsibility of the Coast Guard (originally known as the Preventive Waterguard), whose men were often assisted by local fishermen and naval personnel. Early 1824 saw the foundation of the National Institution for the Preservation of Lives from Shipwreck (now the Royal National Lifeboat Institution). Two of the first official lifeboats were put into service at Studland and Portland in the mid-1820's, but the Portland boat was never used. Portlanders much preferred to launch their trusted lerrets, immensely sturdy craft, robustly designed to withstand the rigours of being hauled up and down Chesil Beach. The local fishermen were also anxious not to lose their salvage rights, for the lifeboat service saves lives, but lays no claim to the vessels it brings to safety. Gradually more Dorset lifeboats came on service and by 1875 they were in use at Lyme Regis, Chapman's Pool and Kimmeridge, Studland and Poole, Weymouth, and Swanage.

The Rocket Apparatus: practice on Chesil Beach during the early years of this century. The original of this alas poor quality photograph was titled the 'Mariners Last Hope'.

A brig ashore. Although the vessel is not named, this scene may well depict the wreck of the *Skylark* at Kimmeridge in 1845.

Not every shipping disaster occurred in the open sea. A particularly tragic event in 1806 saw fourteen people drowned when the Wareham and Poole passage boat ran aground in fog as it entered the river at Wareham. The boat overturned as attempts were made to refloat it and only one man survived. A similar accident had befallen an earlier passage boat in Poole Harbour in March 1759. Heading for Ower, it grounded in wet, freezing conditions and thirteen of the nineteen on board died as they tried to struggle to the safety of Furzey Island across 500 yards of mud.

As the century progressed, newspapers grew bulkier and the reporting of local wrecks more detailed. In April 1845 the stranding of the 10-gun brig *Skylark* on Kimmeridge Ledges caused great excitement and Weymouth's steam packets were called upon to help get her off. Weymouth having just lost the Channel Islands mail service to Southampton, the timing could not have been worse. Two of the three redundant steamers had already left the port and the third had sailed with the mails on its final run to Guernsey and Jersey. It was left to the Revenue sailing cutters to hasten to the scene, but in deteriorating weather they were unable to shift the brig. Returning to Portland for the night, the *Eagle* cutter ran aground at Sandsfoot, but was successfully refloated. Despite boats being swamped and limbs being broken, all on board the *Skylark* survived, although their vessel was a total loss. The gales continued, and next morning a large smack was seen to capsize in Portland Race, drowning her five-man crew. In appalling conditions local boats eventually took the *Swallow* in tow, crowds of sightseers lining the pier and quays to see her brought into the Weymouth Harbour.

FAMOUS VISITORS

Crowds also turned out on 10 September 1859 to see the arrival of Isambard Kingdom Brunel's new steamship *Great Eastern*, due at Portland for coaling during her sea trials. Launched at last after innumerable delays, she was then the biggest ship in the world – 700 feet long and 19,000-tons gross. In a vast engineering enterprise employing hundreds of men there had inevitably been accidents and fatalities during her construction and the ship had gathered about

The *Great Eastern* proved uneconomic on the passenger routes. Under the supervision of Sir Daniel Gooch she returned to Portland in the 1860's and 1870's prior to Transatlantic cablelaying voyages.

her legends of ill-luck, added to when Brunel, already a sick man, collapsed on her decks days before his 'great babe' left the Thames.

It was to be a subdued arrival at Portland. Cheers from the shore went unanswered and those with spyglasses soon realised that something was terribly amiss – the ship had only four funnels instead of five. The previous evening a tremendous explosion had blown the forward funnel into the air and ripped through the passenger saloon, fortunately empty at the time. There was momentary chaos as crew and passengers were concussed by noise, blinded by steam and showered with debris.

The human tragedy soon became apparent as a fireman, horribly

Drama as the *Royal Adelaide* struck the Chesil in 1872, coming 'broadside on the beach, the waves hurling her only about 20 yards from the feet of the people who were assembled to render assistance'. Note the flare overhead.

scalded and in agony, threw himself overboard and was crushed by the *Great Eastern*'s huge paddle wheel. Five more were to die of their burns and others were seriously injured. Brunel himself lived for only a few days after learning of this dreadful accident on his great but troubled ship.

The *Great Eastern* was repaired at Portland and a relic of her visit remains in Weymouth today – her discarded funnel was acquired by Weymouth Waterworks Company and installed as a vertical pipe at the Sutton Poyntz works. The local paddle steamer companies were quick to profit from the ship's enforced stay and began running trips across Portland Harbour carrying visitors prepared to pay the two shillings and sixpence admission fee to inspect the *Great Eastern*.

Never a commercial success, the huge vessel was eventually converted for transatlantic cablelaying and revisited Portland in the 1860's and 1870's. Tragedy touched her once again during these later visits when five young local men decided to take a closer look at the famous ship by rowing round her one Sunday morning. Their small boat overturned, drowning three of the lads. It was, commented the *Dorset County Chronicle* sternly, 'a forcible warning to other Sabbath breakers who persist in going boating on the Lord's Day'.

Twenty years later one of America's best-known ships was an unexpected visitor to Dorset's shores. The *Constitution*, popularly known as 'Old Ironsides' was on her way home from France when she ran aground in fog at Ballard Point on 17 January 1879. She was, after several attempts, towed off with relatively minor damage. Built in 1797, the frigate was celebrated for her exploits in the War of 1812, which had included the capture of four British ships. Eventually restored at Boston where she was built, the 200-year-old *Constitution* remains there today, a museum exhibit and tourist attraction.

THE EMIGRANT SHIPS
1872: THE 'ROYAL ADELAIDE'

The iron sailing ship *Royal Adelaide* was Australia-bound when she left London on 14 November 1872, carrying a general cargo (which included a large number of cases of spirits), and sixty-seven crew and passengers. On the afternoon of the 25th she was seen to be embayed in the West Bay, and that evening she struck Chesil Beach broadside-on between Wyke Regis and Portland. Those watching from the shore could do nothing until she was close enough to fire a line on board. Once a cradle had been rigged up the rescue began and in difficult conditions sixty people were brought ashore. It was a dramatic scene, the beach lit by tar barrels and blue lights, and it was watched by hundreds. News had soon spread of the helpless ship off Chesil and the local population sped to the scene, many arriving on the packed 5 pm train from Weymouth on the Weymouth and Portland Railway. As the ship began to break up, the line parted and the last few still on board were swept away and drowned.

If the rescue had enthralled the spectators, the cargo thrown up by the dying ship was to excite them even more, and wholesale looting began. Portlander Robert Otter wrote a poem about the loss of the ship in which he narrated the night's events with great gusto, and described the array of goods which were spread along the shingle:

> . . .*bales of beautiful cloth and silk*
> *And boxes of gloves, made of kid, white as milk;*
> *And boots without number, of all sorts and sizes!*
> *And hats by the thousand, of all shapes and prices,*
> *And ready made clothes of every description.*
> *But of half what was there, you will have no conception –*
> *There were boxes of candles and sweet scented soap;*
> *And cotton by cart loads was soon thrown up.*
> *And knives and forks and all sorts of cans,*
> *And high-dried herrings and fine bacon hams;*
> *And bottles of wine, pale ale, and stout,*
> *And casks of vinegar rolling about;*
> *And chests of tea, coffee, and figs,*
> *Cocks and hens and live and dead pigs . . .*

Coastguards, police and the military could do little to control the crowds and some stolen goods were later buried in gardens to evade the inevitable searches by law enforcement officers which followed. It was quite a night and next morning the roll call in at least one local school was abandoned as most of the children had joined their parents treasure-hunting on Chesil Beach.

Sadly, the tubs of spirits coming ashore were to cause the deaths of three local men and a young lad who fell asleep drunk on the wet, cold stones:

> *But while some were plundering and carrying things home*
> *Others were busy in drinking the rum*
> *While some with pebbles soon knocked the head in*
> *Of the big brandy tubs and the casks of gin;*
> *For they felt themselves cold and thought it no harm*
> *To have a good drink to keep themselves warm.*
> *But alas! poor souls, they drank rather too deep*
> *Of the brandy and rum and soon fell asleep*
> *In the wind and the rain, to lie all the night*
> *In a drunken state and an awful plight.*

'In the meantime a lifesaving apparatus had been rigged up, consisting of a life buoy and a kind of bag into which the person about to be rescued had to sit.' Survivors from the *Royal Adelaide* being brought to safety.

At the end of it all, the *Royal Adelaide*'s captain had his certificate suspended for twelve months for having misjudged his course whilst attempting to round Portland Bill and seek shelter in Portland Roads. It had been yet another year when end of November gales brought disaster to shipping off the Dorset coast. Two days prior to the wreck of the *Royal Adelaide*, a little Welsh schooner, the *Jane Catherine* was smashed to matchwood within minutes of striking Chesil Beach and before any attempt could be made to rescue her crew of four. Next day, the smack *Courier* foundered near Charmouth. The crew of the North Shields vessel *Cassibelaunus* were picked up by the Lyme lifeboat, their barque foundering near Fleet on the 26th. Continuing into December, the storms drove the full rigged German ship *Stralsund* on Kimmeridge Ledges, where Kimmeridge lifeboat took off her crew. Many more storm damaged vessels that week were forced to seek the shelter of Portland Roads.

One eyewitness to the attempts to blow up the *Forest* wrote: 'A puncheon containing about 240lb of gunpowder was then submerged and fired . . . Its explosion resulted in the uprising of some forty feet of a beautiful cascade of water, and the untimely death of a few over venturesome fish.'

At Portland, on a site which fittingly overlooks the Channel, stands a memorial to those who died in its stormy waters in 1877. St Andrew's Church, Southwell is known by all as 'Avalanche Church'. The *Avalanche* was a New Zealand bound iron sailing ship. She sank following a collision on the night of 11 September 1877, taking with her sixty three passengers and all but three of her crew.

In murky, worsening weather conditions, two ships were bearing down the Channel that night, the *Avalanche* and the *Forest*, a wooden sailing ship, in ballast and bound for New York. Each became aware of the other vessel's lights, but the fact that they were on a collision course was realised too late and the *Forest* struck the *Avalanche* amidships several times with such force that she practically cut the iron ship in two. In the moments after the impact three of the *Avalanche*'s crew scrambled into the bows of the *Forest*. The two ships parted and the *Avalanche* went straight to the bottom. Fearing that she would also sink, all on board the *Forest* took to three boats, only one of which remained afloat the following morning.

Portlanders awoke to find Chesil Beach strewn yet again with the wreckage of a disaster at sea. In appalling conditions fishermen launched lerrets into the surf and a chain of rescuers stood ready on the beach. All twelve in the *Forest*'s single surviving boat were brought to safety; one hundred and eight lives had been lost. It was a tragedy which left the small New Zealand town of Wanganui devastated, for many of its citizens were returning home on the *Avalanche*.

The derelict *Forest* remained afloat, partly submerged and a danger to shipping. The Navy was called in to destroy the wreck but several failed attempts using explosives left her even higher out of the water than before. Weymouth and Portland Steam Packet Company's paddlers began running excursion trips out to the scene where amused passengers watched an ironclad and three steam launches' unsuccessful efforts to blow up the wooden hull. Eventually the Navy towed the *Forest* further down the Channel and blew it to pieces on 22 September.

An advertised excursion to Torquay on 27 August 1886 attracted many to Bournemouth Pier and they duly boarded the *Bournemouth*, a paddle steamer belonging to the Bournemouth, Swanage and Poole Steam Packet Company. When she left for the trip along the coast the *Bournemouth* had more than 200 people on board: of whom only forty-five could be carried in her three small lifeboats and one dinghy. The Weymouth steamer *Empress* ran the same trip from Bournemouth that Friday. The Torquay visitors enjoyed their day out and embarked for home in the late afternoon.

By then a dense sea fog had descended and at around seven in the evening the *Bournemouth* struck hard on the rocks at Portland Bill. Fortunately the sea was calm, for once some of the women passengers had been taken off the wreck in the *Bournemouth*'s boats, more than 160 were left behind awaiting rescue. Conditions being favourable, all were ferried off by local boats; had a heavy sea been running, the stranding of the paddle steamer could well have become a major tragedy. At the subsequent inquiry it was suggested to her captain that he might have been racing the *Empress* home. Although he blamed the incident on compass error his certificate was suspended for twelve months 'for travelling at 16 knots in dense fog on a miscalculated course'.

Despite considerable press comment on the overloading of the paddle steamer and lack of adequate lifeboat accommodation, it was to be another twenty-six years before the question was really addressed, and action was only then prompted by the appalling death toll when the *Titanic* went down in 1912.

The wrecking of the *Bournemouth* at Portland Bill in 1886 provoked much comment in the national press regarding the overloading of small coastal pleasure steamers. The *Daily Telegraph* reported that 'the *Bournemouth* had almost as many passengers on board her as she had tons of burthen.'
'But the beautiful 'Bournemouth' has parted in two;
Her work is now done; her years have been few;
She's a wreck on the rocks, for already the bell
Of the once splendid boat has tolled her death knell.'
(from a contemporary poem by Portlander Robert Otter)

A year after the fortunate escape of the *Bournemouth*'s passengers, a poignant entry appeared in the log book of Holy Trinity Boys School, Weymouth. It reads: 'A deep gloom rests on the managers, teachers and town generally on account of the loss of ten residents of the town who were drowned on Sunday morning by the wrecking of a yacht on the Breakwater.'

The yacht was the *Laureate*. She belonged to local boatbuilder Edward Lewis Carter who had taken a group of friends and acquaintances on a conger fishing trip. It was late October and the weather prospects weren't good, but the *Laureate* successfully reached Portland, where she moored half-a-mile from the Breakwater. Some of the twelve on board grew anxious about the increasing storm, but it was judged safer to remain moored rather than attempt a run for shelter. By morning there were only two survivors to give an account of what happened that night. The mooring rope either snapped or became unfastened with the result that the *Laureate* drifted onto the Breakwater. Some of the fishermen climbed into the small boat which had gone out with the yacht, but as it was in danger of being smashed against the *Laureate* they attempted to get back on board. In this manoeuvre some were drowned. Others lost their lives as they tried to scramble onto the Breakwater. Ten died: eight were married men who left, 'Three widows and ten children totally unprovided for and eight widows and 29 children desolate'.

The closing years of the nineteenth century saw a succession of sailing vessels and steamships lost all along the Dorset coast. Some wrecks were spectacular and seen by all; the loss of others went almost unnoticed. In August 1894 the screw steamer *Gertrude* grounded in fog at Blacknor, Portland. In a calm sea, all on board were rescued before the *Gertrude* provided, as do many wrecked ships, dramatic shots for the local photographers as she slipped deeper into the water. Yet just a few months earlier all that had been found when the Inverness schooner *Lord Duffus* was lost at Portland Bill were bodies, pieces of wood and part of a sodden ship's log, which provided the only clue to its identity.

The years 1849 to 1872 had seen the construction of the first two arms of Portland Breakwaters, then intended to give complete protection to the harbour of refuge at Portland. Advances in submarine and torpedo warfare found the two-mile stretch of water between Breakwater Fort and the Weymouth mainland open to attack and in the 1890s work began on building the two Bincleaves Breakwaters, a project which took some ten years to complete.

On 13 February 1899 the 1200-ton Liverpool steamer *Stuart* broke adrift in Portland Harbour during a heavy gale. She veered dangerously close to other shipping before striking the unfinished breakwater works. Here a sudden huge sea washed her right over the top and swept her ashore at Preston Beach, north of Weymouth, where she remained firmly lodged for six weeks before being refloated.

Vessels striking the breakwaters were a not infrequent occurrence, but there was a particularly unhappy incident in the closing days of 1900. The 3000-ton *Enecuri*, a Spanish steamship, dragged her anchors and grounded on the rocks close to Breakwater Fort on 28

Wrecked wooden ships were often pounded to pieces by the sea within hours or days. Iron vessels survive rather longer: the remains of the steamer *Gertrude* still lie off Blacknor, Portland, more than one hundred years after she ran aground.

The *Stuart*, swept over the unfinished Portland Breakwater works in 1899, ended up ashore between Preston and Osmington. Refloated weeks later, she made it back to Portland under her own steam.

December. Soldiers from the fort assisted all twenty-six on board to safety. Later in the day several of the crew returned to the ship, but next morning the *Enecuri* slipped off the Breakwater and sank. All those on her decks leapt to safety, but her captain apparently made no attempt to escape. His skeleton and that of his pet dog were found in the cabin three years later by divers working on the wreck.

WAR

If gales had not ended their journey first, Dorset's earliest known shipwrecks – a fleet of Danish galleys wrecked off Peveril Point in 877 – could well have been casualties of war. The Danes had left Wareham to relieve their countrymen besieged at Exeter by King Alfred's forces, but storms drove 120 of the Danish vessels on shore before English war galleys had a chance to intercept them.

It was the sixteenth century which brought to England one of the most famous of all fleets – the Spanish Armada. In the waters off Studland lies a sunken warship which was once part of that historic naval force. The Portuguese carrack *San Salvador* was damaged by fire and explosions on board during the battle off Portland between the English and Spanish flotillas in July 1588. 'Much splitted and torn', the captured prize was brought into Weymouth. At around 900-tons she was too big to enter harbour and lay in the Bay whilst instructions were awaited from the Admiralty as to her fate, and that of her armaments and stores.

The townsfolk had no doubts about what should be done with the contents of the Spanish prize, rowing out in small boats and helping themselves. These raids and the authorised removal of some of her munitions left the carrack light in the water. When some months later it was decided to remove her to the Royal Naval Dockyard at Portsmouth, the *San Salvador* sailed only as far as Studland before she turned turtle and sank, drowning more than twenty of those on board.

Another famous sea fight which resulted in the loss of warships off the Dorset coast took place in the seventeenth century. During the Battle of Portland in 1653 the 32-gun *Sampson* and several Dutch ships were sunk before the English under Blake chased Admiral Van Tromp's Dutch fleet up the Channel to eventual defeat.

But it is the two World Wars of the twentieth century which

Twenty one years old, and after a total commissioned service of eighteen years, HMS *Hood* is positioned at the southern entrance to Portland Harbour prior to being deliberately sunk as a blockship in November 1914.

account for the vast tonnage of vessels and hundreds of lost lives which now lie at the bottom of the English Channel. More than 150 ships are known to have been torpedoed, mined or bombed off Dorset in the wars of 1914-1918 and 1939-1945 and the casualty lists are not complete. At the time these shipwrecks rarely made the news due to wartime press restrictions, and a fear that reporting their loss might prove useful to the enemy.

One huge battleship was inadvertently sent to the bottom of Lyme Bay in the months before World War I broke out. The superstructure of the obsolete 14,000-ton *Empress of India* was being used for target practice when she was accidentally holed below the waterline, causing her to turn over and sink. A second Victorian battleship was sunk, this time deliberately, soon after the war started. It had been realised that Portland Harbour's South Ship Channel entrance was vulnerable to enemy attack and in November 1914 HMS *Hood*, stripped of her fittings, was positioned across this sizeable stretch of open sea between the breakwaters and sunk to block it. She, too, turned over as she went down and remains there to this day, her keel visible at low water.

The story of a third battleship which lies off the Dorset coast is a tragic one. HMS *Formidable* was torpedoed and sunk in Lyme Bay in

January 1915, at a time when the threat posed by German submarine activity in the Channel had not yet been fully realised.

The 5th Battle Squadron, under the command of Vice Admiral Sir Lewis Bayly, C-in-C of the Channel Fleet, was out on the last day of December 1914 on firing exercises which were intended to continue next morning. At nightfall, in bright moonlight, the squadron was sailing in line ahead, with *Formidable* in the rear. She was torpedoed at 2.30 am on New Year's Day, 1915. Her assailant was the patrolling U-boat U-24 and the British battleship sank after a second torpedo struck. There was a heavy sea running and it was bitterly cold. More than 500 of her complement of 780 men were lost that night, and some were to die in the ship's boats after having been adrift almost twenty-four hours in freezing winter weather before they were found.

Today, in the quirky way that some historic events are remembered, it is a headstone in Abbotsbury Gardens which prompts many to enquire into the story of the *Formidable*. The stone marks the grave of the captain's dog 'Bruce', whose body was washed up on the nearby beach the day after the battleship went down. A second dog

HMS *Formidable* was an early victim of a German submarine attack in the First World War. More than 500 lives were lost when she was torpedoed on the first day of 1915.

Lassie, the cross-bred collie who helped save the life of a
seaman from the *Formidable*.

also has a part to play in the story of the *Formidable*. A supposedly dead sailor washed up at Lyme Regis was lying in the Pilot Boat inn. But after being licked for half-an-hour by the landlord's rough-haired collie, Lassie, it was realized that the man was still alive. Reports of his survival reached Hollywood, inspiring the creation of the now immortal sheepdog that still bears Lassie's name.

U-boat activity intensified and from late 1916 until the autumn of 1918 not a month passed without British shipping being lost off Dorset through enemy action. Not every German submarine survived and between Portland and Start Point U-85, UB-19, UB-72, UB-74, UC-51 and UC-62 were sunk. The area's last British casualties of World War I were two merchant steamships attacked on successive days in September 1918. On the 14th the *Gibel Hamam* was torpedoed by UB-103 off Abbotsbury with the loss of twenty-one of her crew. The *Ethel* fell victim to UB-104 a little farther to the west and sank whilst under tow for Portland.

World War II was to begin quietly for mainland Britain, the first few months of inactivity becoming known as the 'Phoney War'. Little was happening inland apart from intense defence preparations, but those living on the Dorset coast soon had evidence that German submarines had been busy laying mines in the English Channel.

Less than two weeks after war had been declared, survivors from the *Alex Van Opstal* were landed at Weymouth. The Belgian passenger liner had sunk after striking a mine five miles east of the Shambles lightship on 15 September 1939. The Dutch steamship *Binnendijk* was next to fall foul of mines in the same area, and her loss was followed by that of the Greek vessel *Elena R.*

These ships went down unseen from the shore, but the aftermath of the area's first serious air raid was witnessed by many. Early on the morning of 4 July 1940 twenty Luftwaffe planes flew low over Portland Harbour and released their bombs, scoring direct hits on an auxiliary anti-aircraft vessel, HMS *Foylebank*, a converted former merchantman. It was a devastating attack and the ship was ablaze within minutes. Those who lived locally at the time vividly recall the pall of dense black oily smoke which hung in the air and drifted along the coast from the dying ship. Leading Seaman Jack Mantle was mortally wounded in the raid but stayed at his post,

Part of a painting by John Hamilton showing Stukas dive-bombing the
Foylebank, in Portland Harbour on July 4th 1940.

repeatedly firing his gun at the enemy aircraft. For his gallantry in
this action he was posthumously awarded the Victoria Cross.

That same month German attacks on Channel shipping resulted
in the loss of the liner *Aeneas*, the motor vessel *Dallas City*, the
steamships *Deucalion*, *Elmcrest*, *Kolga* and *Hartlepool*, HMS *War-
rior*, a converted luxury yacht, the destroyer HMS *Delight*, and
the *Meknes*, a French liner. The merchant ship *Hartlepool* almost
made it to Weymouth after being hit, but finally sank just outside
the harbour close to the Mixen rocks. Her superstructure was
clearly visible, but it proved a target for enemy bombers and was
removed some weeks later. The sunken vessel remained an obstruc-
tion near the harbour entrance until she was removed in the early
1950s.

Channel convoys continued to be harried by enemy aircraft, surface craft and submarines until the final weeks of war in 1945, the
last vessel being lost off Dorset in February that year. She was the

steamship *Everleigh*, torpedoed by U-1017 and sunk with the loss of six of her crew.

World War II had seen the appearance in Dorset of vast numbers of Landing Craft as LCTs and LCIs (Tank and Infantry Landing Craft) began assembling for the Invasion force. These were the vessels which played a leading role in the D-Day landings of June 1944 and they were designed with bow doors and ramps which slammed down on beaches to enable men and machines to storm ashore. Practice had to make perfect. The Dorset/Devon coast became the backdrop to endless rehearsals for the real thing – one of which was to have tragic consequences. A convoy of LCs heavily laden with American troops and vehicles was out in the Channel during Exercise Tiger in April 1944. When twelve miles off Portland they were torpedoed by German E-boats, prowling the area in search of Allied shipping. Two craft, LSTs 507 and 531 were sunk, and the sea was soon littered with the bodies of the US servicemen who had been on board. It was a disaster which cost more than 500 lives.

Dorset's involvement with the D-Day invasion forces continued for many months after the successful landings in Normandy, and landing craft were a familiar sight around the coast. Many were beached on Weymouth sands for repairs, and they ran back and forth across the Channel taking out men and supplies and returning with the dead, wounded and prisoners of war. One of the craft, LCT (A) 2454, got into difficulties off Chesil in October 1944 and was the scene of a heroic rescue close to Portland. Nine of those on board were swept away and drowned as she struck the shingle. Two, injured, reached the shore. Two ratings were left clinging perilously to the wheelhouse on board the craft. Coastguards repeatedly tried to reach the vessel with a line but they were overwhelmed by gigantic seas which drowned Commander J. A. Pennington Legh and Coastguard Treadwell. A third coastguard was pulled clear. A young member of the rocket crew, Portlander George Brown, then battled through the surf to get a line on board. He succeeded in reaching and saving the two Navy men on the craft, later receiving an award for his gallantry. At times of exceptionally low tide today the remains of the old LCT are exposed in the Chesil pebbles and the wind whistles eerily through her now paper-thin metal plates.

MODERN TIMES

The years which led up to the outbreak of World War I had seen the end of an era as sail gave way to steam, but although steamships predominate in the long lists of Dorset's twentieth century shipwrecks, some very fine sailing ships also came ashore.

The last of the big sailing ships lost on the Dorset coast was the French vessel *Madeleine Tristan*, wrecked at Portland in September 1930. On voyage from Lorient in Brittany to Le Havre, severe gales blew her hopelessly off course. Her captain ran her skilfully up the beach in what was described as 'a regular grandfather of a sea', at Chesil Cove, on what he at first assumed to be the north coast of France. He and his crew of six were soon rescued but the ship slewed round in the continuing gales and was to become a total wreck. She lay in the Cove for five years and provided authentic location shots for scenes in a feature film, a host of tall stories about the size of the rats on board (she was carrying 50-tons of grain), and plenty of firewood for the Islanders when she was eventually broken up around Christmastime 1935.

Two sailing vessels which got into difficulties on the west side of Portland were wrecked on successive days in October, 1903. Tugs went to the aid of the Latvian vessel *Emma Maria*. She had left Teignmouth for Lisbon carrying china clay. In worsening weather conditions it proved impossible to tow her to safety and she was left anchored at Blacknor. She dragged her anchors in the increasing gale and was driven on Chesil Beach. As her mainmast snapped it fell across the beach, allowing her crew to scramble to safety.

Sightseers who turned out next morning to view the wreck found another ship heading straight for the beach. In freshening winds the Norwegian *Patria* had lost her sails and was unable to round Portland Bill. Her captain decided his best chance was to run the barque onto the shingle and gave the order, 'Sea boots off and every

Surely the most photographed of all the vessels which have come to grief on Chesil Beach, the *Madeleine Tristan* remained beached in the Cove for five years after she was wrecked in 1930. 'She was,' recalled a local fisherman, 'the finest prettiest sailing ship ever to come ashore on these coasts.'

The Latvian *Emma Maria*, laden with china clay, was a total loss in 1903.

man for himself!'. As she struck, some of her crew jumped into the surf, others were rescued from huge seas after a line was got on board. One of the young crewmen saved was A.H. Rasmussen who, many years later, recalled the rescue in his autobiography *Sea Fever*: 'One moment I was riding on the crest of a huge comber and then it would suddenly break under me and hurl me headlong into a welter of boiling surf and shingle, suck me back, lift me up and toss me down again. How long I was tossed about I don't know. I only remember dimly that I saw a man running towards me through that deadly surf with a rope round his waist. The next moment a great cheer came from the beach as he grabbed me, and dozens of willing hands hauled us in'.

Rasmussen's obvious affection for the *Patria* provides a fitting tribute to the fine sailing vessels of a bygone age: ' . . . her designer

Opposite page Some idea of the violence of a Chesil storm is contained in a newspaper report of the wreck of the *Patria* in 1903. 'The copper sheathing had been torn like wallpaper from the vessel's bottom by the fierce beating of the waves and the pounding on the beach, and great sheets were blown hither and thither by the gale, flashing with a sheen as of hammered gold.' The lower photograph shows Chesil Cove littered with her cargo of timber a few days afterwards.

The 3,500-ton Russian steamer *Cerera* was en route for Odessa when she grounded at St Aldhelm's Head in 1907. Tugs got her off and towed her to Portland.

All on board were rescued when the *Montanes* stranded in fog at St Aldhelm's Head in November 1906. The steamer was carrying silver ores, manganese, canary seed, cork, wine – and oranges, hundreds of which floated on the surface of the sea the morning after she was wrecked.

'In the meantime, the fog had lifted and a rapidly increasing crowd on the cliffs saw all that was going on.' The *Bulow*, stranded in fog at Portland in June 1914, was successfully refloated.

The *Patroclus* could be counted as one of the lucky ones, despite being stranded at Portland on Friday the 13th of September, 1907! The combined efforts of five salvage tugs got her off just over a week later and there was no loss of life. Cosens and Company's *Queen* is shown alongside.

must have realised she would probably be the last sailing ship he would build, and he had lavished all his love and skill on her, so that the new generation of steamshipmen could see what a thing of speed and beauty a sailing ship could be'.

In the first half of this century numerous steamships came ashore. Some were successfully refloated, others became total losses. Salvage work was a lucrative activity during these years. Competition was fierce and news of a stranded vessel sent local tugs scurrying to the scene. Cosens and Company's paddle steamers, more usually associated with holiday pleasure trips, are frequently to be found busily occupied in photographs of Dorset shipwrecks.

It was dense fog, rather than rough weather, which brought the majority of steamers to grief. At St Aldhelm's Head alone the Spanish *Montanes* was wrecked in November 1906, the *Cerera* in 1907, the *Ilona*, a steam yacht, in 1909, the *Envermeu* in April 1914. There were similar strandings in fog all along the coast. One or two are unusual and of particular interest.

The *Bulow* was certainly an unexpected visitor at Blacknor, Portland, in June 1914. The large German liner was on her way from Yokohama to Southampton with more than 300 passengers on board when she struck. Her siren brought most of Portland's inhabitants to the clifftop and when the dense fog lifted they gazed with some amazement at this magnificent vessel in Mutton Cove. Athough the liner did not appear to be in any immediate danger, all her passengers were swiftly taken off and conveyed to Weymouth railway station to continue their journey by train. The speedy evacuation of the ship was no doubt influenced by a shocking maritime disaster which had occurred two weeks earlier in Canada. Following a collision in the St Lawrence Seaway, the liner *Empress of Ireland* had gone down, drowning more than a thousand on board. Included in that number were Weymouth jeweller John Vincent and his wife who had been homeward-bound after visiting relatives in Quebec. Fortunately there were no casualties on the *Bulow* and she was successfully refloated. At almost the same spot the 5000-ton *Patroclus* went ashore in 1907, the *Okahandja* in 1910 and the *Turenne* in 1913 – all were towed off. The *Myrtledene* in March 1912 was less fortunate. Badly holed, she became a complete loss.

A real scoop for Weymouth photographer Graham Herbert. His night-time shot of the Union Castle line's *Winchester Castle* is the only record of the liner's brief stay at Portland in 1936.

Fog brought a second liner ashore at Blacknor in February 1936. Fewer people saw the night-time visit of the *Winchester Castle*. Owned by the Union Castle line she was on the last leg of a voyage home from South Africa. Stuck on rocks for just a few hours, she refloated on the next tide, and was soon on her way to Southampton with 300 passengers still on board.

A third luxury liner almost became a casualty off Dorset in 1933, but it was another of the great hazards at sea – fire which caused *L'Atlantique* to veer towards the English side of the Channel. Ablaze, and drifting helplessly she was shadowed by a French minesweeper, ready to sink the burning ship if she became a real danger to other shipping. Hundreds watched the drama. The liner was red-hot above the waterline and giving off dense clouds of black smoke. She was not carrying passengers but 17 of her crew of 230 lost their lives in the incident. Eventually French tugs took her in tow for Cherbourg, averting one Dorset shipwreck.

A more recent victim of fire off the Dorset coast was the Libyan freighter *Ebn Magid*, seen by millions on the television news, and by many in Weymouth and Portland from their windows as she blazed in Portland Harbour at the end of January 1986. The fire was successfully brought under control.

Some fine ships end their lives usefully, if a little less exaltedly than their careers of former years. Famous liners of the leading shipping companies often went into retirement as coal hulks in the years when the Navy relied on many thousands of tons of coal to fuel its fleets. One of these suffered the dubious distinction of being twice sunk in Portland Harbour. She was the *Haytian*, built in 1875 and owned in her prime by the West India and Pacific Steam Ship Company. In 1910, laden with 3000-tons of coal, she was rammed amidships and sunk by the SS *Nymphaea* close to the 'Hole in the Wall', the South Ship Channel between the breakwaters. Raised, the *Haytian* stayed on station until February 1937 when the Royal Navy's patrol vessel HMS *PC* 74 of the Anti-Submarine Flotilla suffered a steering gear failure and rammed her yet again. This time the hulk and her 4000-tons of coal were raised by Weymouth salvage expert Louis Basso. Another former crack liner, the *Himalaya*, once the pride of the

The *Haytian*, a former liner, was sunk and salvaged twice whilst serving out her retirement as a coal hulk in Portland Harbour. She is seen here in her glory days as a luxury passenger steamship on the West Indies route in the 1870's.

So close, so calm – yet thirty six men had died trying to reach the shore
when giant seas swept the *Treveal* onto the treacherous Kimmeridge
Ledges in January 1920.

P & O fleet, was 87-years-old when a stick of German bombs ended
her days as a coal hulk during a World War II air raid on Portland
Harbour. Close to the breakwater where she sank during a gale in
1935 lies a third hulk, the *Countess of Erne*, a paddle steamer
which had started life in the late nineteenth century on the regular
Holyhead-Dublin run.

Gales continued to bring ships on shore and one of Dorset's most
tragic shipwreck incidents of this century occurred on a stormy night
in 1920. The 5000-ton steamship *Treveal* stranded on Kimmeridge
Ledges, appearing in the calmer conditions of the following day to be
deceptively close to the shore and safety. Yet 36 of the 43 men on
board lost their lives on the night of 9/10 January.

It had been from the start an unhappy story. Laden with jute and
ore and bound from Calcutta to Dundee, the *Treveal* had called at
Portland to pick up a pilot; none being available the agent had
instructed her captain to proceed without one. Driven off course in
heavy weather the ship struck the Ledges. A searching tug failed to
find the vessel and by the time Weymouth lifeboat, an oared craft,

The stranding of the *Preveza* in 1920 provided some dramatic shots as she lay broadside on in Chesil Cove, Portland.

had been towed through mountainous seas to aid the *Treveal* she had been abandoned by her crew. In those terrible conditions only seven reached the shore alive. A sequel to these events was the dismissal of the officer in charge of the St Alban's Head coastguard station for failure to report the vessel's condition and position to the proper authorities. Two years after the *Treveal* was lost, the salvage tug *Glenmore* sank after striking the wreck, and thirty-two years later another salvage vessel, the *Abide*, ran aground whilst working at the site and had to be towed off. In the villages of Dorset today there are older residents who can still recall the *Treveal*'s salvaged cargo of jute being laid along the hedgerows to dry out.

Just along the coast a week later two vessels were lost on successive days, this time without casualties. The Greek steamer *Preveza* was already well-known at Portland. She had called to collect coal and stores before continuing a voyage to Cardiff, none of which had been paid for. On reaching the Welsh port she was refused cargo as it was discovered she was not insured. Intending to head up the Channel for Rotterdam she drifted ashore in fog on 15 January and grounded broadside on in Chesil Cove. Portland was the last place she wanted to revisit, and the local firms whose bills for provisioning remained unpaid immediately nailed writs to the mast to prevent her leaving. The *Preveza* never did leave the Island in one piece. Although conditions were calm at the time of her stranding and there were high hopes of getting her off, the weather deteriorated. A salvage tug, the *Ellida*, got into difficulties and was almost wrecked alongside the Greek vessel. Heavy seas soon destroyed the *Preveza* as she lay in the Cove, where her two forty-ton boilers remained for sixteen years before they were finally broken up and removed.

Next day, 16 January, Portland fisherman Albert Saunders, known by his local nickname of 'Sunny', heard a distress siren at Blacknor. In the darkness and continuing fog he climbed over a mile of dangerous rocks to reach the stranded Admiralty trawler *James Fennell*, only to find he was cut off by the sea from reaching the wreck. Undaunted, he retraced his steps, climbed the steep cliff and descended it again from the opposite side. This enabled him to get within hailing distance of the vessel, which had been bound from Portsmouth to Gibraltar with sixteen on board. Having waded waist

Still lying below the rocks at Portland today, the Admiralty trawler *James Fennell* was the scene of a dramatic rescue operation in January 1920. The vessel sank shortly after salvage work began.

deep into the sea to secure a line thrown by the crew, Sunny then directed the entire rescue operation, bringing 15 men ashore before the captain, last man to leave, fell from the line and was rescued by Sunny and the crew. The local press rightly described Sunny Saunders as a man of 'courage, perseverance and determination'. Salvage work began on the *James Fennell* but shortly afterwards the trawler slid off the rocks and sank.

Submarine losses swell the lists of Dorset's shipping casualties in the twentieth century. One very early 'submersible' was reported to have been involved in an accident in Poole Harbour in the mid-nineteenth century when six men were said to have narrowly escaped with their lives. The vessel is not identified but it could possibly have been an unsuccessful trial of Charles Babbage's 'Submarine apparatus for the explosion of vessels', which was under-going tests in the 1850's.

Dorset's first documented peacetime submarine loss was that of L24, sunk in collision with HMS *Resolution* off Portland Bill on 10 January 1924. Time runs out quickly for those trapped in undersea craft and there was little hope for the 43 men on board. 'Rescue operations are proceeding with feverish haste but these are being hindered by the unfavourable weather conditions, which are very bad in the exposed part of the Channel'. All were lost and the sub was never raised. One of those on the same Channel exercise that day was the submarine M2, herself to be lost off Portland eight years later.

Submarines M1, M2 and M3 had originally been laid down as K18, K19 and K20 in the K-boat series of ill-fated vessels notorious for the tragic accidents which befell them. The M-boats were of a revolutionary design; they carried an enormous 12 inch gun mounted on the hull and their appearance was fearsome. Completed in 1918, the M's were outlawed in 1922 by the Washington Naval Treaty which restricted submarines to guns of 8 inch calibre. M2 was converted as a submersible aircraft carrier. A watertight hangar was constructed on her deck and a Parnall Peto seaplane made successful

Sombre commemorative postcards were published in memory of those who lost their lives when ships went down. This postcard was published when the submarine L.24 sank with all hands in 1924.

Submarine M.2, the first submersible aircraft carrier, complete with the hangar which housed her folding-wing biplane, and its launching catapult. Her 3-inch anti-aircraft gun can also be seen. The M2 sank in 1932.

flights from the sub. Then on 26 January 1932 it was announced that, 'News has been received this evening that Submarine M2 dived at about 10.30 this morning off Portland and since then no further communication has been received from her'.

Nothing was ever heard again from M2. It is thought improperly closed hangar doors caused her to founder that morning. The wreck was located and although attempts were made to bring her to the surface, only one body was recovered before salvage was eventually abandoned and today M2 lies on the seabed, her crew entombed. M1, still armed with her great gun, had already been lost in a collision off Start Point in 1925. M3, converted as a minelayer, was scrapped in 1932.

The post-World War II years saw the loss of two submarines at Portland. In September 1945 the French *Minerve* drifted ashore at the Bill after a tow parted. She sank, without loss of life. Those on board the *Sidon*, lying alongside the depot ship HMS *Maidstone* at Portland Harbour in 1955, were less fortunate. Fuel leaking from an experimental torpedo caused a tremendous explosion on board and fire took hold. Two officers and ten ratings were killed when the *Sidon* sank, and Surgeon Lieutenant Rhodes of the rescue party died of asphyxiation as he tried to help others to safety. The submarine was raised but was sunk intentionally off Portland two years later as an Asdic target.

Portland Harbour had witnessed another naval tragedy in 1948. A pinnace of HMS *Illustrious* left Weymouth Harbour in the late

It is perhaps fitting that the final photograph should be of one of Dorset's more modern lifeboats, Weymouth's *Tony Vandervell*.

evening of 18 October, taking fifty-one liberty men back to the aircraft carrier. The boat was overloaded and it was blowing a gale but the pinnace ploughed on, only to founder fifty yards from *Illustrious*, drowning twenty-nine of the returning sailors.

Today, mercifully few ships are lost along the Dorset coast. Modern communications systems, state of the art technology and efficient rescue systems are in place to prevent most tragedies. Unpredictable weather and an untrustworthy sea will always lie in wait though, and their combined power was well-demonstrated in the gales of October 1996 which tore an oil rig from its moorings and hurled it across Portland Harbour, where it struck, and fortunately wedged against the Breakwater. The sea has a will of its own and as long as man is prepared to pit his skills against wind and tide there will, inevitably, be more names to add to the already long lists of Dorset shipwrecks.

FURTHER READING

More than one thousand vessels are known to have been wrecked or stranded along the Dorset coast. Accounts of many of these incidents can be gleaned from local newspapers of the eighteenth, nineteenth and twentieth centuries.

LISTS OF DORSET SHIPWRECKS

Boddy, Maureen, *Dorset shipwrecks*. A series of shipwreck articles and wreck lists published in *Dorset – The County Magazine*. Issues 48, 49, 50 and 55. 1975-76.

Larn, Richard & Bridget, *Shipwreck index of the British Isles. Volume 1: Isles of Scilly, Cornwall, Devon, Dorset.* (Lloyd's Register of Shipping), 1995.

GENERAL WORKS

Burnett, David, *Dorset Shipwrecks* (Dovecote Press), 1982.

Farr, Grahame, *Wreck and Rescue on the Dorset Coast: the story of the Dorset lifeboats* (D. Bradford Barton Ltd), 1972 (individual histories of several of the Dorset lifeboat stations have also been published).

Hinchcliffe, John, *Dive Dorset* (Underwater World Publications Ltd), 1984.

Shovlar, Steve, *Dorset Shipwrecks : a comprehensive guide to the shipwrecks of Purbeck and Poole Bay* (Freestyle Publications), 1996.

Smith, Graham, *Hampshire and Dorset Shipwrecks* (Countryside Books), 1995.

EIGHTEENTH CENTURY

'A Gentleman in the Neighbourhood,' *An authentick account of the* Hope . . . *cast away on Portland Beach in the County of Dorset.* 1749.

Francklyn, Thomas, *Serious advice and Fair Warning to all that live upon the sea-coast of England and Wales.* London, 1756.

Meriton, Henry and Rogers, John, *A circumstantial narrative of the loss of the Halsewell,* 8th ed. London, 1786.
A true and particular account of the loss of the Halsewell, East Indiaman, London, Sabine, 1786.

Smith, Charlotte, *Narrative of the loss of the Catherine, Venus, Piedmont, Transports, and the Thomas, Golden Grove and Aeolus, Merchant ships, near Weymouth,* 1796.

NINETEENTH CENTURY

Burgoyne, G.A., *A correct narrative of the loss of the Earl of Abergavenny, East Indiaman*, Weymouth (Virtue), 1805.

'A Gentleman in the East India House', *An authentic narrative of the loss of the Earl of Abergavenny*. 4th Ed. 1805.

Pocock's *Authentic narrative of the loss of the Earl of Abergavenny, East Indiaman*, 1805.

TWENTIETH CENTURY

Davison, Ann, *Last Voyage* (Heinemann), 1953. (An account of the loss of the yacht *Reliance* at Portland in 1949).

Rasmussen, A.H., *Sea Fever* (Constable), 1952. (The loss of the *Patria* on Chesil Beach in 1903).

ACKNOWLEDGEMENTS

I would like to thank Ed Cumming and the Chelmsford Underwater Archaeological Unit, Edwin Kestin, Ruth Lawrence, Derek Whatmoor, Dorset County Library and the Weymouth RNLI for kindly allowing me to reproduce illustrations in this book. The photograph of the *Tony Vandervell*, Weymouth's lifeboat, was taken by Mr D.R. 'Nobby' Clark. The extracts from *Sea Fever* by A.H. Rasmussen are quoted by kind permission of Constable.

The

DISCOVER DORSET

Series of Books

A series of paperback books providing informative illustrated
introductions to Dorset's history, culture and way of life.
The following titles have so far been published.

All the books about Dorset published by The Dovecote Press
are available in bookshops throughout the county,
or in case of difficulty direct from the publishers.
The Dovecote Press Ltd, Stanbridge,
Wimborne, Dorset BH21 4JD
Tel: 01258 840549.